HEALED

PASTOR YOUMONE BERRIEN

Copyright

National Snow and Ice Data Center (2019).
https://nsidc.org/cryosphere/quickfacts/icebergs.html

Heslop-Harrison, John. "Germination." Encyclopedia Britannica,
Encyclopedia Britannica, Inc., 21 Dec. 2018,
www.britannica.com/science/germination.

Cover Design and edit by Mayuni Karr

For bookings or media inquiries, contact:

Public Relations Manager:

Mayuni Karr

Contact Information:

commissionedbcoc@gmail.com

Pastor Youmone Berrien

DEDICATION

To the strong ones-- the living inspirations of God's ability to heal every manner of sickness and disease; the ones that have touched God's heart and mine:

Kat, Nap, and Rose

"We are like common clay jars that carry this glorious treasure within, so that the extraordinary overflow of power will be seen as God's, not ours."
2 Corinthians 4:7 TPT

"The word that came to Jeremiah from the Lord: "Arise, and go down to the potter's house, and there I will let you hear my words." So, I went down to the potter's house, and there he was working at his wheel. And the vessel he was making of clay was spoiled in the potter's hand, and he reworked it into another vessel, as it seemed good to the potter to do. Then the word of the Lord came to me: "O house of Israel, can I not do with you as this potter has done? declares the Lord. Behold, like the clay in the potter's hand, so are you in my hand, O house of Israel."
Jeremiah 18:1-6 ESV

We are the cracked clay jars once crafted by the Master Potter but marred by the experiences of life--fragile clay jars purposed to hold the dynamic power of God, now cracked by the pangs of seasons of pain, waiting to be restored again. We have been poured in and poured out, emptied and ready to be filled again, desiring to have the consequential cracks of sin forever filled and cemented shut.

We are limited human vessels at the hands of a limitless, omnipotent God, vulnerable and anxiously waiting to be healed.

Pastor Youmone Berrien

CONTENTS

INTRODUCTION

"And Jesus went throughout all the cities and villages, teaching in their synagogues and proclaiming the gospel of the kingdom and healing every disease and every affliction" (Matthew 9:35 ESV)

One of the more tragic wounds I received happened when I accidentally slammed my thumb in the rear door of our SUV. I was in a rush to get the kids in the house and was not paying attention when I pressed the automatic close button on the truck remote. The force of the door closing jammed my thumb in the corner of the door and I was unable to release it. After visiting the doctor and receiving stitches to close the wound, I started observing the healing process.

My finger-- swollen, discolored and tightly stitched together-- looked dreadful and was writhing with pain. For days I nursed my wound, cleaning the area around the stiches and changing gauze pads soaked with blood. It was disgusting. It wasn't long before I started noticing a callous forming over my wound. It was nothing for which to marvel, rather gaze in disappointment at the less than glamorous white and brown tough skin that scarred my thumb. I began realizing much of the healing process happened under the skin, beneath the callous. So, the hard, unappealing surface of the wound was actually a protective layer that safeguarded and supported what my body was doing to restore what was afflicted. It was during this process that I understood how God, our Jehovah-Rapha, heals...from the inside out.

We come to God afflicted, wounded from immediate and past afflictions—times in our lives where we have been severely cut to the core by an absent parent, molestation by a close relative, failed relationships, job rejection, and the list goes on. It is at these moments in our lives that God initiates the healing process, but He begins the work on the inside of us and it eventually manifests outwardly.

That's the most misunderstood part of His work: we don't realize that the healing we so desperately pleaded for has begun and it looks drastically different from that which we imagined. When God begins a work of healing inside of us, he activates the process of exposing the agents of defilement. How does this process look? It looks and feels like being under a microscope—where every microcosm of your being is examined and evaluated for its effectiveness, leading you closer to the purpose and positioning prepared for you since the beginning of time.

Those areas of defilement—areas that make us unfit for the fight--are exposed and surgically removed by the Chief Surgeon. Those areas are manifested in our patterns of speech, our response to adversity, perception of self-worth, articulation of purpose, and overall assessment of our present condition. What needs to be unearthed in our lives are exposed by God, requiring us to 'deal with' the issues we've persistently and fervently tried to ignore.

God purposes to fully eradicate the defilement and restore you, making you whole again. The Apostle Peter encourages us, "And after you have suffered a little while, the God of all grace, who has called you to his eternal glory in Christ, will himself restore, confirm, strengthen, and establish you" (1 Peter 5:10, ESV). That's what our good and gracious God does for us, He restores, confirms, strengthens, and establishes us back to a place of completeness—no longer broken and defiled, but HEALED.

The Word of the Lord foretold that "He was wounded for our transgressions, He was bruised for our iniquities; The chastisement for our peace was upon Him, And by His stripes we are healed" (Isaiah 53:5 NKJV).

"Therefore, if the Son makes you free, you shall be free indeed" (John 8:36 NKJV). So, be free from sin and its consequences. Walk in the victory fought for you, without shackles, restraints, and crippling instruments because we are now healed and set free from...

HEALED

FEAR

"Now Jabez was more honorable than his brothers, and his mother called his name Jabez, saying, "Because I bore him in pain." And Jabez called on the God of Israel saying, "Oh, that You would bless me indeed, and enlarge my territory, that Your hand would be with me, and that You would keep me from evil, that I may not cause pain!" So God granted him what he requested.

1 Chronicles 4:9-10 NKJV

Jabez, marked at birth with a name that was a constant

reminder of the pain he gave his mother upon entering this world, made special requests of the Lord: that he might be blessed, that his reach might be extended, that he be led, that he remain protected and that he not be a stumbling block for someone else. *Seems like too much to ask at one time right?* Wrong.

Sometimes we limit our requests to God in fear. Fear of rejection, fear of unworthiness, fear of failure and fear of success arrest our faith and muzzle our mouths. There are many instances in which we, as believers, yearn to ask God in prayer for the manifestation of a personal desire, vision or ambition but table our requests in fear that we lack the qualifications, insight, or connections to efficiently carry out such a great task. We ask, " *Who am I that I might do this great thing?*" Insecurities latch on to confidence and distort our thinking, causing us to doubt the voice and direction of the Holy Spirit.

I've often wondered why God chose me to accomplish specific tasks, as unworthy and unprepared as I felt. I was appointed to a top-level position in my profession—one that required me to advise and lead in areas I had minimal formal experience. I considered declining the offer to accept the position for fear that everyone would see how unqualified I truly was for the position, but I heard the voice of the Lord affirm that He was qualifying me for a special assignment He set aside just for me. I learned that it wasn't about whether I was qualified but whether I would allow God to do a work in the earth through me. I'll admit, I was not completely qualified...and that laid the foundation for God to do what He does best.

The point at which we second guess our ability to complete a specific task on our own and highlight our inadequacies is the point at which we release the glory of God to reign in our lives. That's right; we need to second guess our abilities and highlight our inadequacies because the only way we can do anything is through "Christ that strengthens [us] (Philippians 4:13)", not by our own might or ability. Accept the fact that we are not great, indeed, to carry out a great work...but remain confident in knowing that our God is.

What gave Jabez the confidence to ask God for something as large as increasing his possessions and influence, even though he knew he was marred from birth? His confidence in the God who would perform this miracle on his behalf; it was never in his ability to do it for himself. Had Jabez allowed the painful circumstances of his birth-- which named him—orchestrate the events of his future, he wouldn't have possessed the boldness to make such a request to His God. He would have lived in fear of causing pain to others and even himself, crippling his walk into the unrestrained opportunities that awaited him.

God's direction and promises have not changed but our perspective must. There is nothing wrong with asking the Lord for multiple, even great, blessings; the fallacy is presented in the expectation of receiving it in your own strength and for your own benefit. James records that "You ask and do not receive, because you ask amiss, that you may spend it on your pleasures (James 4:3)". How often do we ask God for what gratifies our flesh and glorifies that which displeases Him?

Healing Heart:

What are you asking God for that seems too big, too great, and too far out of reach?

Realm of Self-Surrender

The answer to our request is in the realm of self-surrender. When we truly relinquish our innermost desires and detach from the emotional and spiritual cords that bind us to a life of self-gratification, we will gain an understanding of that which pleases God and receives His approval...which leads to answered prayers. Remember when Jesus was on the boat?

"On that day, when evening had come, he said to them, "Let us go across to the other side." And leaving the crowd, they took him with them in the boat, just as he was. And other boats were with him. And a great windstorm arose, and the waves were breaking into the boat, so that the boat was already filling. But he was in the stern, asleep on the cushion. And they woke him and said to him, "Teacher, do you not care that we are perishing?" (Mark 4:35-38)

"Do you not care that we are perishing?" The disciples asked Jesus whether He was concerned with their perceived demise. Much of fear is an individual's perception of a threat. A deeper look into the text reveals deep truths of the position in which the disciples

---

Much of fear is an individual's perception of a threat.

---

were placed.

Jesus invited those to whom He was intensively training to

journey with Him to the other side of the sea. Only inviting those He had chosen, he left the crowd at the bank of the sea. What we fail pay attention to is the fact that other boats accompanied them on the sea, as they were conducting their usual fishing business.

Why would Jesus invite his most precious cargo on board a ship that would sink?

Ask yourself the same question: why would the Lord lead me out into the waters of faith to permit my demise? The answer is simple: He wouldn't.

Jesus commandeered the disciples to join him on the boat to cross to the other side. Their fate floated off the tongue of Christ and should have become the bridge of faith over the sea's troubled waters. But, instead those fate filled words were forgotten in the middle of the sea—in the middle of the storm.

In His Storm

The image of the aftermath of a major storm can be discouraging, even depressing. Those who have experienced a major storm understand the overwhelming fear, anxiety and uncertainty moments before, during, and after the storm.

I remember witnessing the devastation of one of the major storms that touched down in central Florida. Residents described sitting in their tubs with their hands over their heads, embracing their children as cyclone force winds ripped through their communities tearing off their roofs, sending debris flying everywhere, snatching building edifices, and toppling walls of homes and businesses. One distraught homeowner described the sense of hopelessness as she stood in what was once her living room, now a pile of timber, and looked out into the neighborhood that had become the evidence of her hard work in making a loving home for her children. She saw nothing but torn down houses and broken-down dreams.

Consoling those who have experienced such a loss requires not only empathy and compassion, but wisdom. Wisdom to know that in the midst of total devastation, God is yet working out all things for our good. While it may feel and appear to be utter destruction around, know that there is a divine purpose at work.

In reflecting on the spiritual storms that I've encountered in my life, I began to understand the delivering power of God concealed in the outer winds of the storms my family and I faced. Those winds packed enough power to demolish any size building that lay in its path. To some, that is discouraging, even depressing, because those buildings that were demolished provided covering, shelter, and protection.

For others, those buildings represented what they had accomplished, the successes, the victories, all they had given birth to that manifested before their eyes. Lastly, to some, those buildings were built by others and encapsulated them, preventing future growth and blocking a clear vision of what lay beyond the barriers before them. To them, the demolition provided hope. Hope to see a future beyond the boundaries in front of them.

The latter set of individuals represent the season in the

believer's life when God is perfecting our ability to wait for His promises to manifest and free us to walk in His purpose for our lives. Many of us labor in this season for longer than desired periods of time (while some of us remain in this season today). In this season, perception meets reality and the wall that others build around you, begins to consume you and block your vision. You can no longer see the hope that lies ahead, the race you've committed to complete, or the crowd of witnesses continuing to cheer you through your struggles. You only see the walls that are stacked in front of you. You become imprisoned by the walls they built. It is God who comes in and tears down the walls freeing you to see the endless possibilities that await you.

The Psalmists wrote, "You've gone into my future to prepare the way..." (Psalms 139:5 TPT). We're reassured that we serve "... a God who does what is right, and [who] smooths out the path ahead of [us]" (Isaiah 26:7 NLT). How might the Lord enter our future to prepare a way for us? How might He clear our paths? By sending storms.

Sending storms seems like an odd solution to clearing a path, doesn't it? Imagine an architect tasked with building a massive, technologically advanced structure on the grounds where a current run-down building sits. The plans for the new structure are already prepared and the architect is ready to begin building this new project, but first must get the old building and any other structures that are not in the new development's plans out of the way. A major storm brews in the ocean and finds its way to land, toppling the old

building that held the ground hostage, freeing the architect to now
come in with his crew to conduct an easy clean of the clutter and
begin the building process. Was the storm a blessing, in this case, or

---

"[God] is omnisciently aware of the plans that He has crafted for our lives."

---

a curse for the architect? A blessing—some would say in disguise, but
we believe, divine.

How else does one demolish an edifice that is blocking the
path of a road being constructed; by destroying what sits idly or
intentionally in the way. God never promised to do it the way our
human reasoning sees fit, but the way that best fits the plans He has
prepared for our lives. "For My thoughts are not your thoughts, nor
are your ways My ways," says the Lord" (Isaiah 55:8 NKJV) and He
reminds us in Jeremiah 29:11 that He is omnisciently aware of the
plans that He has crafted for our lives.

Choosing joblessness as a method of clearing my own path
would appear reckless, careless, irresponsible—especially with a
family of small children and major financial obligations. Removing a
formal job from the picture seems disastrous. But what if I told you
that this caring and loving God demolished that sturdy edifice and
caused my husband and I to stand looking at its ruins? Would you
still believe this God to be just that: caring and loving, even all-
knowing and powerful? Would you still acknowledge Him as

responsible and in control if I told you our bank account dwindled from $2000 to $25 and then to "faith" in those days of demolition?

There we stood, waiting for the dust of joblessness and financial scarcity to settle, holding on to every promise we read in God's Word.

Healing Heart:

What sits idly or intentionally in your way, preventing you from being who God has purposed you to be? How has God demolished or removed these obstructions out of your path?

_____

_____

_____

_____

_____

_____

_____

_____

_____

_____

_____

We were encouraged by the word of the Lord saying, "But forget all that— it is nothing compared to what I am going to do. For I am about to do something new. See, I have already begun! Do you not see it? I will make a pathway through the wilderness. I will create rivers in the dry wasteland" (Isaiah 43:18-19, NLT).

□□□

□□We tend to get stuck on the demolition of what we were so comfortable seeing that its destruction consumes our thoughts and chokes our hope, breathing life into our greatest fears. The Lord said, "forget all that!" Stop dwelling on the process of your deliverance and praise in advance for its product. Product over process. Do you really need to know 'How' God did, as long as you know THAT He did it? We only are privy to the 'why's' of God's miracles to deepen our understanding of His grace, mercy and love for us. So, if we hardly need to know the 'why's', why are we pressed about knowing the 'how's'?

Product

Process

Forget the destruction, stop comparing it to the new thing He is doing before your eyes. What you've gone through can't be compared to where He's taking you and what you will see. It can't be compared because it's new; something you've never seen before.

Clear the Cache

God clears our faith caches so our
spiritual storage can hold the new
downloads of His grace.

A cache is a computer memory used for storage of
frequently or recently used instructions or data. Just recently I was
building a website for my business and got locked out of the web
builder site. After discussing the issue with the Tech Support team, I
was given specific instructions on how to clear the caches. They
walked me through it and explained the importance of doing this
every so often to avoid the computer storage from getting bogged
down with old downloads and information. Once I cleared our
cache, I was able to begin again creating my website.

The same thing happens spiritually. Our storage becomes
full with past failures, fears, heartaches, and disappointments, to the
point that we can no longer operate efficiently. We must clear our

cache. For some, it's a simple reset and for others, it's a guided step by step process that requires intense support. But, to begin creating again and building something new, the old downloads must be cleared.

Clear the cache so comparison won't blind you to what God is doing in your life.

One of the most powerful messages I received from the Lord was, "See, I've already begun; do you see it?". I hadn't seen it. I was so consumed with the visual of the storm's aftermath that I didn't see the vision—the clear path that lay ahead of me. Instead of looking forward at the hills and mountains I could now see because what had previously obstructed my view was gone, I looked down at the rumble of debris.

What swept up my anxiety was the fact of God's word that He had already started this "new thing". So, during the destruction, I could rest assure that every piece of crumpled concrete was a part of His plan...because He had already started working the plan.

Release the need to allow fear to take a foothold in the plans God has for your life. As disciples of Christ, we've been led onto a vessel that will function to transport us from one place not the next. We have been assured by Christ that the assignment or task that awaits us is on the other side of the sea. So, if storms arise, we should rebuke the fear that pervades knowing that the storm(s) are unable to stop the plan of God has on our lives.

"For you did not receive the spirit of slavery to fall back into fear, but you have received the Spirit of adoption as sons, by whom we cry, "Abba! Father!"-Romans 8:15 ESV

Healing Heart:

What has life downloaded into your 'faith cache' that needs to be cleared out? (Be specific)

Cementing the Cracks

Take a step towards being healed from FEAR by engaging in the reflection activity below.

Read: Psalm 23:4, 1 Peter 5:7, Deuteronomy 31:6, Isaiah 41:10, and Isaiah 54:4

Respond: How is God clearing the clutter and removing the debris of your past?

_____

_____

_____

_____

_____

_____

_____

_____

_____

_____

_____

_____

_____

_____

Release: Write a message of praise for the product God is producing in your life.

_____

_____

_____

_____

_____

_____

_____

_____

_____

_____

_____

_____

_____

_____

_____

_____

_____

_____

_____

_____

Prayer:

Lord, let the circumstances that once marked me, make me a testament of your grace and favor. Enlarge my reach in Your kingdom so that you may be glorified the more. Remove fear and anxiety so that I am unafraid to walk in the calling and plans you have for me. Teach me to be thankful for the storms of life that provide opportunity for my demonstration of faith. Clear the clutter of my memory and help me look at the things that You are doing in my life as a blessing and a step in the process of my healing. In Jesus's name, amen.

HEALED

UNBELIEF

"And Jesus said to him, "'If you can'! All things are possible for one who believes." Immediately the father of the child cried out and said, "I believe; help my unbelief!" And when Jesus saw that a crowd came running together, he rebuked the unclean spirit, saying to it, "You mute and deaf spirit, I command you, come out of him and never enter him again." And after crying out and convulsing him terribly, it came out, and the boy was like a corpse, so that most of them said, "He is dead." But Jesus took him by the hand and lifted him up, and he arose. And he said to them, "This kind cannot be driven out by anything but prayer."

(Mark 9:23-27, 29 ESV)

In Mark 9, a father brings his son to be healed from demonic attacks that violently overtake the young boy's body, nearly killing him with each attack. At his wit's end, the father begs Jesus to help him if He was able to do so, commenting that his initial request to the disciples was unproductive. Seemingly insulted, Jesus resoundingly replies, "What do you mean, 'If I can'? Anything is possible if a person believes" (Mark 9:23, NLT). With that one subtle rebuke, came the moment of transparency—a moment we all must embrace to manifest true healing—the father confirmed his desire to believe, but admitted he needed help fighting the spirit of unbelief that took residence in his body throughout the years.

Just think, this father dealt with his son's illness all of his son's life.

He had probably taken his son to multiple doctors, seeking treatment of various forms, just for all to conclude that there was nothing they could do for him. Then, he hears of a man from God that possesses the power to heal and had given the same healing authority to his disciples; but when he brings his son to the disciples, they also could not heal the boy.

> ## "The disappointment of one expectation breeds examples of subsequent disappointments."

So, what happened to this man's belief that the teacher of these disciples possessed the power to do what they could not do, but was imparted by Him for them to do? This is the birth of unbelief. The disappointment of one expectation breeds examples of subsequent disappointments. To be healed, we must interrupt and destroy the cyclical nature of this phenomenon.

Why don't we believe the prophetic word spoken over our lives? Why is it so hard to believe that one has received the promises of God? Our belief in the prophetic word of God reveals the condition of our heart towards God. Do we truly believe the report of the Lord questioned by the prophet Isaiah? Or do we believe that which we can see, feel, or perceive to be the reality of our position?

Unbelief becomes the spiritual manifestation of one's confidence in the omnipotence of God. *Is He, indeed, all powerful and able to respond to the needs of His people without the assistance or interference of man?* When viewed from the scope of this inflammatory question, the act of unbelief is blasphemous and a direct insult to the character and nature of our loving God. How can those who declare to be children of the Most High God second guess His ability to confirm and carry out that which He has spoken. If for no other reason than the record of the process of Creation through God's spoken words, we should believe that what He speaks manifests.

Life and Death

The enemy attempted to use my testimony to legitimize his attack.

On February 27, 2014 I was admitted to the hospital and prepped for life-saving surgery after Emergency Room doctors diagnosed me with a ruptured Ectopic pregnancy resulting in internal bleeding. After four hours of surgery and the removal of a Fallopian tube, I laid in my recovery room grateful for God's mercy and protection, baffled by the events that had just transpired. I had no clue; there was no indication, no warning, that death had attempted to enter my body. I conducted life as usual, until life nearly escaped me...and that was the reality that the enemy used in his attack.

My testimony, preached in pulpits throughout 2014, revealed the three proceeding weeks following my surgery that led me back and forth to the emergency room with threats of cardiac abnormalities and possible blood clots, all associated with the events of February 27th.

I preached about Christ's power to heal all the afflictions that threatened to thwart the call of God on my life. I stood before congregations of women and shared what it was like facing death, not fully realizing the closeness of death until it's exit from my hospital room. I spoke about the prayers I offered up on the hospital bed, even while floating in and out of consciousness. All of this made for an impactful testimony and successful altar call when posing the question to all who would hear, "so, will you give your life to Christ knowing that this may be your final opportunity?".

My testimony touched hearts, changed lives, and shined light in the dark places of the soul. But, I, the minister of the Gospel, remained afflicted. I didn't believe I was completely healed. I preached about being healed, reminded others that they were healed, quoted scriptures about being healed...but was not mentally healed myself. Parishioners were unaware of the constant battle I faced daily—fighting the mental battle waged against me from the enemy. I was continuously reminded of the events that occurred on February 27th. *How do I know if I'm sick like before? Has my heart healed from that murmur they heard? Why am I so tired, is something wrong? What if there is a blood clot; how will I know? How will my boys take it if I pass away? What will my husband do if I leave here?*

Worry led to anxiety and anxiety led to multiple trips to the doctor's office, only to receive the results that I was in good health: no murmur, no clots, no blood disorder...nothing wrong. But I couldn't accept it.

Days of worry transcended to months of anxiety. I became the friend of "urgent care" facilities, going back and forth with symptoms I diagnosed as abnormal and life threatening. There was no walking forward into my healing, only sideways shuffling so that I could more aptly drag the bags of burden and uncertainty with me along this journey of life.

I constantly prayed for deliverance. I wanted to receive the prophecy and promise of my healing. I wanted to feel normal once again...and when I had resolved to do so, the enemy attacked again. After determining to try out our new health insurance, my family and I scheduled wellness appointments with our primary doctors. I confidently participated in the routine wellness examinations knowing I was healthy and had no abnormalities. Well, at the close of my examination, my doctor informed me that she was concerned about what appeared to be a lump on my thyroid, (similar in appearance to an Adam's Apple). She informed me that while common in women, it could be a sign of Thyroid Cancer, as one of her patients was diagnosed with cancer after having his large lump examined. She said the word nobody wants to ever hear uttered from their physician's mouth, *cancer.* She nonchalantly referred me to a well-known cancer hospital in my city for an ultrasound examination of my thyroid.

In those three weeks of waiting for the ultrasound appointment, I battled with the mental manifestations of every symptom I read during the course of my research of thyroid disease. I envisioned my hands shaking uncontrollably, heart palpitating, vision blurred, inability to swallow, and labored breathing. I pondered radiation treatment and thyroid removal surgery, even death...unjustified conclusions drawn by fear and faithlessness. In perpetuation of these unfounded assumptions, the enemy used the voice of a childhood friend to intensify his attack. I was warned and prepped by this longtime confidant of the possibilities of contracting Grave's disease, blood clots, and dying of subsequent heart disease as this friend's loved one faced years before.

It wasn't until I heard the voice of the Lord speak through my associate (who doesn't profess to be believe in Christ) that "everything is fine! Nothing is wrong with you! It's all in your head", I began to understand that I had the power over the works of the enemy. *"Behold, I give you the authority to trample on serpents and scorpions, and over all the power of the enemy, and nothing shall by any means hurt you (Luke 10:19)".*

I fasted and prayed, asking the Holy Spirit to renew and refocus my mind daily. Yet, I still anxiously awaited the call from the doctor's office, and when the call was delayed, I called the office myself. I initially rejected the practitioners reporting of the results asking her to confirm my name and the location of the hospital the examination took place, (as I refused to believe the results were mine). She repeated the doctor's report that my thyroid was normal and functioning properly...no lump, no mass. So why was it so difficult, even after I began reconditioning my mind to receive the confirmation of my physical healing? Because the manifestation of healing begins in the mind...and my healing had not yet manifested.

Healing Heart:

What bags of burden are you dragging from season to season?

_____

_____

_____

_____

_____

_____

_____

_____

_____

_____

_____

_____

_____

Twin Nature

So, why is it so difficult to believe you're healed and made whole? Why is it so difficult to believe the report of doctors, even believe the report of the Lord? The answer is mysteriously hidden in the revelation of the duality of our human nature.

The Bible records a revelatory example of an individual struggling with twin nature.

John 20:24-25 ESV records, "Now Thomas, one of the twelve, called the Twin, was not with them when Jesus came. So the other disciples told him, "We have seen the Lord." But he said to them, "Unless I see in his hands the mark of the nails and place my finger into the mark of the nails, and place my hand into his side, I will never believe."

Thomas, also known as Didymus the Twin, was an apostle of Christ famously known for his refusal to accept the report of the other apostles regarding Christ's resurrection. Absent the day Christ appeared to the disciples, Thomas made the resounding declaration that he would not believe until he saw the resurrected Christ himself, verified by the evidence of what He saw done to Jesus on the cross. He knew he saw them nail him to the cross and stab a spear in his side to ensure his demise, so Thomas held to the rubric of his reality and would not alter his belief regarding the fulfillment of the word preached to them over the past years. Even though Jesus prophesied to them that once his body (the temple) was destroyed, he would rebuild it in three days (John 2:19), Thomas

The Rubric of our Reality:
A checklist of expectations and
value placeholders that illustrate
our perspective of a situation.

refused to believe.

Thomas's twin nature, the habit of being both a believer and doubter, dismantled the solid foundation the Master Teacher built during His years of discipleship. The Book of James declares that, "A double minded man is unstable in all his ways" (James 1:8, KJV). Thomas was, indeed, unstable in his belief in Christ's ability to perform what He had always professed: His resurrection and power over death. Perhaps he permitted the disappointment of his absence at Christ's initial appearance to the disciples to steal his hope and confidence in the fulfillment of God's Word?

Healing Heart:

What traumatic experience has caused you to doubt what you whole-heartedly believed?

----

*Have you ever allowed disappointment to rob you of
knowledge that would move your faith forward?*

Prior to my current professional appointment, I was an educational consultant working exclusively with school districts, administrators, and staff at schools facing various challenges. I loved working with this population and experienced great success. It wasn't until I was not selected as the chosen candidate for a position I greatly desired that I began second- guessing my professional calling. I rejected the testimonials of administrators and staff whose practice was transformed as a result of the work we had done together, and received the word spoken by someone close to me that I was unqualified for the next level of promotion...which was contrary to the word the Lord had previously spoken to me. I allowed the disappointment of not being selected to steal the seeds of promise that could have moved my faith beyond rejection into divine selection and appointment.

Here I was, trapped in the duality of my humanness, just like Thomas.

The Passion Translation of the Bible records that eight days after initially appearing to the disciples in Thomas's absence, Jesus appeared again, but at a time when Thomas was present. This time, Christ exposed and confronted Thomas's doubt by satisfying his created rubric expectations. He invited Thomas to put his finger in the visible hole in his hand and the wound in his side. He invited Thomas to physically touch what his faith could not see.

"Then, looking into Thomas' eyes, he said, "Put your finger

here in the wounds of my hands. Here—put your hand into my wounded side and see for yourself. Thomas, don't give in to your doubts any longer, just believe!" (John 20:27, TPT).

How often do we give in to doubt—allowing it to run our lives, control our emotions, and regulate the realities we choose to believe?

Jesus' rebuke to Thomas came at a point in Thomas's life when Thomas's faith had taken a major hit. His confidence in Christ was at an all-time low after seeing the one to which held his adoration and devotion, crucified on a sinner's cross. The residual effects of major attacks on our faith are visible in our willingness to believe that which is inconsistent with what we've seen.

Healing Heart:

How have the effects of major attacks on your faith impacted your willingness to believe?

Pastor Youmone Berrien

Thomas needed to be healed from the perception of what he had seen. Instead of filing Christ's crucifixion in the failure folder, he should have labeled it "V" for victory for Christ's victory over death and victory for those that would believe in the future because now all who believed would become heirs to the Kingdom of God through Christ.

When we begin to associate that which is a disappointment to our flesh as necessary for the activation of God's plan in the earth, we change the reality of our experience and align our beliefs to the purposes of God. Now, the concept of healing can manifest in our lives, because doubt no longer reigns.

Environment

Some of our healing comes when we leave our dwelling place of unbelief. The gospel of Mark records an incident in which the townspeople of Bethsaida brought a blind man to Jesus to be healed. While the visible need was for restoration of his physical sight, Jesus began the healing process with touching the man's hand and delivering him out of the city infamously known for being unrepentant and rebellious.

"And they came to Bethsaida. And some people brought to him a blind man and begged him to touch him. And he took the blind man by the hand and led him out of the village, and when he had spit on his eyes and laid his hands on him, he asked him, "Do you see anything?" (Mark 8:22-23, ESV).

While those close to this man could be applauded for caring enough to bring him to Jesus, they were careless enough to continue living in an unrepentant state, while expecting the flow of the promises of God to manifest in their lives. Jesus rebuked the entire city due to their refusal to acknowledge their fallen state, confess their sins, and believe in Christ's ability to restore their fellowship with God (Luke 10:13). They rejected the truth of their condition.

How many of us are living in environments that are opposed to the truth of our condition? A response to this question takes into consideration the environments represented in our lives-- our physical, emotional and financial surroundings. An environment opposed to the truth of our condition is one that fosters the false sense of security we possess in our ability to continue hiding behind masks of deceit. These environments nurture a false self-righteousness and independence that is enmity to God's will for us. God cares about the truth. He desires, by His Spirit, to lead us to an environment of truth, not a lie.

Are you living in a lie? Are you confined to the cocoon of deception pretending to be well but dying inside? These questions should be posed in examining every environment in our lives.

Healing Heart:

What environments do you currently reside that is not conducive to your healing?

Physically, where are you? Are you in a temporary location meant to prepare you for your permanent residence? Have you become comfortable in a temporal locale? If so, God may be transitioning you away from your place of familiarity and complacency. My family and I moved to the Panhandle of Florida after years of living in my hometown. It was a tough transition, as I left many friends, family, and professional connections. But I later realized the need to heal from my past hurts and disappointments.

The Lord transitioned us to a temporary haven for our healing where we experienced success in ministry, professionally, financially, and emotionally. Whereas miscarriages consumed our reality in my hometown, I gave birth to a healthy son in my Panhandle holding place. I thought this place of healing would be my family's final destination but made it clear that he only led us there for our healing and preparation for this next season of our lives. We were comfortable and loving life, because we were now healed from our hurts, but God determined to elevate us into our purpose and lead us out (once again) to a different environment. I learned to embrace divine mobility.

Embrace divine mobility.

Financially, where do you stand, in relation to what is owed and your sources of income? I'll honestly admit, my financial health was in a more destitute state than I was willing to admit to myself. After multiple repossessions and delinquencies due to spontaneous and unplanned purchases, my credit score took a more than 200 point hit and left me credit unworthy. I was advised to seek a financial advisor for assistance with repairing (healing) my finances and transforming my financial stewardship, but I refused to even pull my free credit report to become aware of my true financial status. So, I kept spending and kept making on-the-fly decisions without facing the full scope of my decline yet kept praying for deliverance and restoration of my finances. My prayers and declarations were incongruent with my financial decisions. I was living in a bubble of a lie and it wouldn't be until the bubble exploded that I would be free to confront the reality of my negligence and path to financial freedom.

Are you free to confront the reality of your negligence?

Emotionally, how stable are you and how well do you respond to situations that arise? The time to slow, stop, and exit the emotional rollercoasters of life is now—and it is okay to seek help if you need assistance with doing this. The enemy would have you believe your efforts to seek help, exposing your weakness, is evidence of your failure. But real strength is admitting your weakness and allowing God's grace to be made perfect (2 Corinthians 12:9). I've wrestled with depression and low self-esteem for more than half of my time on earth, and only recently felt comfortable voicing my silent struggles to close friends and clergy. Why was that? My fear of not meeting other people's expectations (and even those unrealistic expectations to strive for perfection set for myself) became my modus operandi. I subjected my joy and peace to the opinions of others and found myself lost in a place of chaos and uncertainty. God's Spirit led me out of this place just as I contemplated ending my life. I let what I felt in the moment orchestrate the volume of voices that guided my day to day interactions and responses, and the voices were literally driving me crazy. So, I began reading God's Words to me-- through His Holy Bible—more than I allowed the voices to speak to me. God's Spirit grabbed my hand and removed me from the emotional solitary confinement that imprisoned me and freed me to be what and who God's word said I was.

The time to slow, stop, and exit the emotional rollercoasters of life is now.

The truth of the matter was that the people of Bethsaida were walking trees: uprooted, fruitless, and wayward. After being led out of the city and having spit placed on his eyes, the blind man told Jesus that he could see people walking before him but as trees walking, not as people walking—a sight contrary to God's expected purpose for nature. God purposed trees to be planted, sturdy, and stable...unmovable. The prophet Jeremiah decreed that one who has developed a firm trust in the Lord would be like a tree planted by a river, with roots that penetrate deep into the earth and spread far and wide to absorb nutrients to be fed and facilitate fruit production (Jeremiah 17:3).

The people of Bethsaida refused to acknowledge their low state of spiritual maturity. Their gaze was fixed on the obvious handicap of their townsman not their own crippling condition. Much of the environmental factors that disintegrate our belief in God, is internal...not eternal. A change in environment can do wonders for our belief in God. But we must be willing to acknowledge our condition and allow God to heal our unbelief.

Much of the environmental factors that disintegrate our belief in God is internal...not eternal.

Declare the prophetic message of the Lord today: I am healed; I am victorious; I am delivered, because I believe.

Healing Heart:

What internal struggles are clouding the vision of your healing?

Cementing the Cracks

Take a step towards being healed from UNBELIEF by engaging in the reflection activity below.

Read: James 1:6, Mark 6:5-6, and Hebrews 3:12-19

Respond: What areas of unbelief lie dormant in your life and possess the ability to cripple your walk in the promises of God?

Release: Write a declaration that expresses your belief in God's love and power to fulfill the great plans He has crafted for your life.

Prayer:

Heavenly Father, I ask that You help me overcome unbelief. Your word reminds me that you have plans for me and those plans are to prosper me and not harm me—plans to give me a future and hope. Your Son came that I might have life and live more abundantly, so I know that You desire me to dwell in peace and live prosperous. Since I know this, I ask that you heal me from not truly believing Your declarations for my life. Let my faith not stand in the knowledge of men, but in the power of God. Let me not question Your ability to perform wonders in my life. In Jesus's name, Amen.

HEALED

DISOBEDIENCE

"Then Jesus gave them this illustration: 'No one tears a piece of cloth from a new garment and uses it to patch an old garment. For then the new garment would be ruined, and the new patch wouldn't even match the old garment. 'And not one puts new wine into old wineskins. For the new wine would burst the wineskins, spilling the wine and ruining the skins. New wine must be stored in new wineskins. But now one who drinks the old wine seems to want the new wine. The old is just fine, they say." –Luke 5:36-39 NLT

One of the hardest acts of obedience I've undertaken was

to leave my church I became ordained in to embark on the journey God had for my life. After serving in the church for five plus years, the Lord spoke clearly to my husband and I and said, "I've commissioned you to a greater work. Be obedient; go...your gift no longer fits inside the box of your current assignment." That's a tough command to fulfill, especially when loyalty gripped us by the arm, arresting and incarcerating us within the confines of our home church.

Disobedience prevents us from breaking the bonds of misplaced loyalty. Oftentimes we remain in situations God has delivered us from because we would rather remain loyal to man than the call of God on our lives. My husband and I established Commissioned By Christ Outreach Church in 2015 with a small group of individuals desiring to worship and serve God (and His people) in a more personal and intimate way. We will admit the following years brought many challenges and tests to our family dynamics, financial status, and health. But we realized that obedience was, indeed, better than any sacrifice we could have made.

When God is unveiling a new thing in our lives it is difficult to walk in the old. New ideas, new dreams, new assignments can't be contained in vessels from previous seasons. If we do, in fact, believe that God is doing a new thing in our lives, we must also believe and accept the new vehicle by which He will use to carry out this new 'thing'. This new vehicle will require adherence to the instructional manual provided by the Creator. It will require a lean in the opposite direction of our understanding and dependency on the omniscient nature of God.

Timing

To be healed from the spirit of disobedience, accept the surety and intentionality of God's divine timing.

The story of Elijah's flight from Jezebel's wrath was summarized in 1 Kings 19: 8-9 (MSG):

"He got up, ate and drank his fill, and set out. Nourished by that meal, he walked forty days and nights, all the way to the mountain of God, to Horeb. When he got there, he crawled into a cave and went to sleep. Then the word of God came to him: "So Elijah, what are you doing here?"

God's Question to Elijah was simple: What are you doing here? In this place, in this state of mind? In this low state of faith? Trembling in the face of your adversary; scared of external forces you can control...what are you doing *here*? In the words of the R&B songstress Deborah Cox, "How did you get here?".

Healing Heart:

How might you be operating in an expired prophetic word from a previous season?

_____

_____

_____

_____

_____

_____

_____

How would you respond if God asked you, "What are you doing here?" Apparently, Elijah had no business nestled in the crevice of a mountain sleeping, hiding, and sulking. God had work for him to do and he sulked. God asked Elijah what he was doing there because he only got THERE by fear, not faith! Elijah feared and had faith in Jezebel's threat that in 24 hours she would kill him so he decided to run and hide.

In what areas of your life have you moved in fear rather than faith?

When asked by God, "Why are you here?" Elijah's response was rich in self-righteousness but limited in scope and accuracy. The reality was that Elijah was hiding in the crook of a cave because he relied on a word spoken to him in a previous season. Elijah was positioned in his place of hiding because he remembered what God told him to do previously. Elijah was operating in human rationale, remembering how God told him to hide before (1 Kings 17:3) after he spoke a prophetic word to Ahab. It's important to note that we can't operate in human reasoning when walking in God's ordination. We must think as God thinks in terms of "seasons" and this was not Elijah's season to hide.

We can't operate in human reasoning when walking in God's ordination.

Ecclesiastes 3:1-8 reminds us of the diverse seasons believers transition throughout the course of life. Accordingly, there is also a time to stay and a time to run; a time to be seen and a time to hide. God had just demonstrated His great power through the prophet Elijah in chapter 17 by swallowing up and consuming the gods of

Baal with consuming fire. Subsequently, this demonstration won the argument of which god was supreme—it was the God of Elijah. So, there was no need to hide anymore. God was publicly doing a new work through the man of God to show all nations His glory.

When we operate in the physical rather than the spiritual, we take ownership of that great work of God and place the burden of its consequences on us, causing us to operate in fear because we recognize how limited and futile our power is. Elijah took ownership and responsibility of the massacre of the prophets of Baal, and consequently ran to escape the punishment of Jezebel. Because Jezebel and Ahab blamed Elijah's hand not the hand of God for killing their prophets, Elijah felt the load of the responsibility, which activated his faith in his own futile power, deactivating his faith in God, causing him to operate in fear.

Healing Heart:

How might you be operating in an expired prophetic word from a previous season?

Consider the divine orchestration of the Lord in Exodus 13. The children of Israel were enslaved by the Egyptian Pharaoh, overworked and oppressed. Our compassionate and ever-present God saw the inflictions of His people and initiated a series of negotiations with Pharaoh to "let [His] people go so they may worship" Him. We know the story: God hardened Pharaoh's heart and many plagues fell on the Egyptians to the point that Pharaoh pleaded for the children of Israel to leave Egypt, so the plagues would cease.

The scripture picks up at the point of the children of Israel's journey via a roundabout route through the wilderness. One might question why God would lead His people into a wilderness or dry and barren land when delivering them from an oppressor? The answer was hidden in the preventative and cautionary care of the Lord.

God is aware of the durability of our faith. The shorter route would lead the children of Israel directly into the land of the Philistines, a land consumed with giants who would have overpowered the frail children of God. God did not lead them through enemy territory at that time because their faith was fragile. How many of us still have fragile faith? The smallest amount of opposition, persecution, affliction, rejection, or heart break causes our faith to fail and we stop being sold out for the Lord. Can you admit to ever having fragile faith?

God is aware of the durability of our faith.

We've experienced moments for which the fragility of our faith was exposed. After listening to the voice of God and relocating to a small town in central Florida, my husband and I experienced a severe financial setback. The Lord had called the both of us to a season of entrepreneurship and total dependency on His provision. In previous seasons there was enough money to meet our needs and even our wants, however, at that season we continuously complained and cried out to God because of the opposition we faced on our jobs. We asked God to deliver us from mediocrity and complacency and entrust us with a vision greater than ourselves. I even remember bargaining with God asking to be a stay at home mom and pastor, devoting my days to ministry and caring for my infant son.

Then July 1st came. Neither of us had a job and thirty days before being forced to move from the apartment my contract job paid for. We sought God and asked for guidance, even a sign to confirm our next steps. My husband's state-issued barbering license confirmed our need to move to his hometown and open a barber shop there, as he would be the only licensed African-American barber in the town. There was a need. God revealed to us that our planting, placement, positioning, purpose, promotion and provision was in the place of the greatest need. We were needed there.

Germination

Germination is the process by which a seed develops into a plant or flower. Spiritual germination is the process by which the seed of God's word grows to maturity producing fruit in the lives of believers. So, in relation to planting, how do you know if the seed you carry is planted in the place of greatest need? The ground or earth has readied the soil to facilitate the process of growth.

The Gospel of Mark referenced the process of spiritual germination sharing that, "The earth produces the crops on its own.

The farmer is expected to do is plant the seed and nurture the ground while the seed transforms.

First a leaf blade pushes through, then the heads of wheat are formed, and finally the grain ripens. And as soon as the grain is ready, the farmer comes and harvests it with a sickle, for the harvest time has come" (Mark 4:28-29, NLT). The earth produces the crop on its own without the knowledge or assistance of the farmer who is responsible for the seed. All the farmer is expected to do is plant the seed and nurture the ground while the seed transforms. □

How does a farmer know if the ground is ready for the seed? A readied or prepared ground has been tilled in a preceding season by clearing the area of impediments like rocks, gravel and grass. Clearing the land of that which might impede growth ensures the effective facilitation of the growth of a seed. Farmers that just drop seeds in the ground without appropriately preparing it are negligent for the stunted growth or death of the seed.

As farmers or carriers of the Word of God, we are responsible for not only carrying, but tilling the soil and planting the seed. We are responsible for preparing the ground to receive the seed through acts of love, gestures of empathy and solidarity with those on the forefront of addressing relevant and impassioned concerns. We are responsible for maintaining and nurturing the ground or earth that holds the seed, even though we have no control over the process by which it grows.

Reflecting on the recent turn of events in my life, my family and I were held in the Panhandle of Florida until the ground prepared for us in Central Florida was ready for planting. We learned a valuable lesson while there: that which is hard to penetrate and unable to enrich may not be ready to receive a seed. Conducting effective ministry was hard...a real battleground.

But we remained faithful to the calling, continued preaching and teaching the Word of God, allowing God to train us for the next phase of ministry. We later realized that God began tilling the soil of the hearts of people to whom we would be sent before sending us with the seed of the Word to our new location. Once we arrived in my husband's hometown, we noticed the favor of God that covered us like a mantle. We moved in and became members of the community, engaged in dialogue regarding the immediate concerns of those in our community and schools, facilitated discussions and empowerment opportunities for our new brothers and sisters, utilized our gifting, talents and insights to impact change in small increments of hope...and most importantly, we loved our new neighbors and community for their uniqueness of which could not be compared to our previous dwelling places. Before we knew it, the seed began producing fruit, there was an interest in seeking Christ and wanting to revolutionize the city for Christ. We were encouraged to facilitate a city-wide revival that would turn our small city upside down (Acts 17:6). The Lord prepared the ground and we were ready to harvest the crops.

Healing Heart:

What dry and desolate situation in your life needs your attention?

_____

_____

_____

_____

_____

_____

_____

_____

Sight and Vision

God positions and plants in the place of greatest need at a particular time. Remember Ezekiel. Ezekiel recorded the infamous exchange and transformation witnessed in the valley of the dry bones. In verse 1 of chapter 37, Ezekiel described the Spirit of the Lord leading him to a valley filled with bones. One might wonder why God would lead his servant to a barren valley experience. *Why would such a loving and caring God subject his beloved to desolation, helplessness, isolation, and defeat?* He wouldn't. The enemy would love us to believe that this valley lacked hope and promise, but it was the total opposite. Ezekiel wasn't alone at all. He was surrounded by an army of individuals that needed his help and his voice.

The Lord juxtaposed Ezekiel's vision against his sight when he asked him if the bones he saw could live again. If Ezekiel responded just from what he saw, he would be justified in emphatically replying, "No!" How could bones that lie in waste in a deserted valley automatically rejoin, develop flesh and marrow, and spontaneously regain life from being dead? Sight would say, "No! These bones could never live again!" But Vision responded with a slightly different outlook, "Only You know, Lord (vs. 3)." Sight responds with its limited view of the physical reality in plain view; Vision responds with an unbound outlook of that which is yet far off but can be attained. Vision says, "I'll work with whatever you give me, knowing You will provide and perform—even if it looks dry now."

Vision responds with an unbound outlook of that which is yet far off but can be attained.

God juxtaposes what exists through faith and obedience with the reality of what can be seen without faith. If we continuously make decisions based on the physical reality that can be seen without faith, we will never be able to fulfill the divine calling of God on our lives, pleasing Him and bringing glory to His name.

Noah was presented with the challenge of walking by faith and Vision and not by Sight.

Remember, without faith, it's impossible to please God.

Hebrews 11:6-7 NLT says, "And it is impossible to please God without faith. Anyone who wants to come to Him must believe that God exists and that He rewards those who sincerely seek Him. It was by faith that Noah built a large boat to save his family from the flood. He obeyed God, who warned him about things that had never happened before. By his faith Noah condemned the rest of the world, and he received the righteousness that comes by faith."

☐☐☐
☐☐☐☐☐☐☐☐☐☐☐☐☐☐☐☐☐☐☐☐☐☐☐☐

Similar to Ezekiel, Noah was presented with the challenge of walking by faith and Vision and not by Sight. He obeyed the voice of the Lord in the midst of looking ridiculous by onlookers. *Who builds a boat in the middle of dry land with no rain in sight?*

Noah was told to build something he had never built or even seen before to safeguard his family from a promise of something he had not yet experienced or seen before. Let's truly understand the complexity of this assignment: God instructed Noah to build an unsinkable vessel during a time when it was unnecessary and unneeded to prepare for something they had never experienced. Noah had never seen or heard of "mist" coming down from the

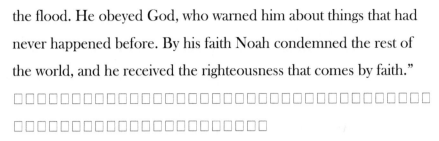

Incongruous Faith—
actions out of alignment with the norm.

heavens, only seeing mist come up from the ground as a result of heat and water from the rivers and streams—so, Noah was building in bewilderment but building in faith. Noah's obedience required his acceptance of the incongruity of what he actually saw and knew to what God commanded and promised. He would be required to possess Incongruous Faith—actions out of alignment with the norm.

Can you imagine Noah beginning construction of a large ship in the middle of dry land and no water in sight? The timing was off. He must have looked foolish to his neighbors, friends, and family. However, while he foolishly and incongruently began building this large vessel on dry land, Noah was obediently walking in divine alignment with God's will for his life and sparing the lives of his entire family.

Has God ever asked you to do something that would be considered incongruous? Has He ever asked you to prepare for something you've never experienced or seen before? Maybe He's asked you to build an unsinkable vessel like a business, marriage, or family that you've never experienced or seen before. Although the task seems incongruent, know that God is leading you further and further away from what you are accustomed to, and directing you into Vision and purpose beyond the frailty of human rationale into the unrestricted will of God.

Obedience to God requires Vision; it requires the humility to recognize one's human limitations and knowledge and surrender to the One who knows the outcomes of His created plans. *Did the rain come?* Yes. *Did it flood?* Eventually. *Were Noah and his family saved from the flood because of his obedience in building the boat?* Yes, in time!

God's timing is perfect and aligned to His will, purpose, and plan for His people and His creations. After nearly 7 months of listening, walking, working, and praying for direction, God released promotion into my life, propelling me to a level of prestige and influence I had never experienced. He held off the creditors and gave my husband and I favor with men until He restored our finances. He provided daily manna (sustenance), strengthening our trust in His ability to meet our daily needs. He deepened our relationship with Him as we learned to walk on water without allowing the distractions of the deep to sink our faith.

We realized one amazing fact: This is His plan that He is working through me; so, I don't have to have the answers or resources...He already has it figured out. So, why not allow Him to lead if He knows the outcome? We were convicted and subsequently healed with an unwavering command: Simply obey.

Healing Heart:

What has God instructed you to engage in that requires
Incongruous Faith?

_____

_____

_____

_____

_____

_____

_____

_____

_____

_____

_____

_____

Cementing the Cracks

Take a step towards being healed from DISOBEDIENCE by engaging in the reflection activity below.

Read: Acts 5:29, Romans 5:19, Deuteronomy 11:8-17

Respond: What is God asking you to do as a measure of your faith that is incongruous to your experience or level of comfort?

Release: Write action steps that will help you prepare the ground to receive the seed God has placed in you.

_____

_____

_____

_____

_____

_____

_____

_____

_____

_____

_____

_____

_____

_____

_____

_____

_____

Prayer:

Holy Spirit, I pray for the realization of the need for a 'new thing' to occur in the body of believers and the release of the 'old way'. I pray for added strength in future endeavors as we begin transforming the lives of this generation. Teach us to be patient and wait for the fullness of time for which you will manifest the plans for our lives. Help us to remain obedient to your instructions even though it may look foolish to man. Give us the vision to see what You see and the confidence to know that all is working for our good and Your glory. In Jesus's name, amen.

UNFORGIVENESS

When Joseph's brothers saw that their father was dead, they said, "It may be that Joseph will hate us and pay us back for all the evil that we did to him." So they sent a message to Joseph, saying, "Your father gave this command before he died: 'Say to Joseph, "Please forgive the transgression of your brothers and their sin, because they did evil to you."' And now, please forgive the transgression of the servants of the God of your father." Joseph wept when they spoke to him. His brothers also came and fell down before him and said, "Behold, we are your servants." But Joseph said to them, "Do not fear, for am I in the place of God? As for you, you meant evil against me, but God meant it for good, to bring it about that many people should be kept alive, as they are today.

Genesis 50: 15-20 ESV

I am guilty of saying, "I'll never forgive (fill in the blank with the name of a person or situation)". I've held unforgiveness in my heart like a prized possession, a thing to honor and revere.

The tables turn when we flip the narrative and place ourselves in the position of one who is in need of forgiveness. What if God chose to hold our transgressions against us and see what we've done to Him instead of the love that He has for us? We would be of a most miserable fate.

In Genesis 50, Joseph had the opportunity to dispense revenge on his brothers, who had rejected, ridiculed, mocked, disowned, backstabbed, and forsaken him. The story is infamous and well-known. A young man, favored by his father, shared his dreams with his siblings and received backlash, unfolding a series of events that would lead him from a pit, to prison, to a palace and position of authority. After many years, the young man has the opportunity to get revenge on his brothers, but instead asked a question many of us should ask when the opportunity to get even presents itself, "Do I sit in the place of God?" *Do I possess the power to condemn you for the wrong you've done to me?* No. God alone—and thanks be to God for that restriction, because we all would have been condemned to a life of damnation long ago.

Joseph realized the underlying purpose in the plots that unfolded in his life, which permitted him to praise God, rather than harbor bitterness and unforgiveness for the people who were vessels to push him into God's purpose for his life.

The Bottom of the 'Berg

Did you know an iceberg is a mountain in the sea? It seems too simple of a concept to think of it as such, but it is.

Research indicates that 90%[1] of an iceberg is below the surface of water. Formed on land and then floating on to the sea

---

What can't be seen, can contribute to the catastrophic ruin of an unsuspecting vessel.

(National Snow and Ice Data Center, 2019). Icebergs are deceptive in that what is seen on the surface is not indicative of the total circumference or scope of the larger concern. The premise remains that what can't be seen, can contribute to the catastrophic ruin of an unsuspecting vessel—in the case of an actual iceberg that vessel would be a ship, however, symbolically, that vessel could be some form of a relationship.

The cliché phrase, "hurt people hurt people" holds true. There were moments in my life in which I would desire, pursue and enter into relationships with friends or romantic partners for the purpose of building something meaningful but was unable because of the icebergs that crowded my sea of emotions. I carried the experiences of past hurts and disappointments to each relationship until I became 'bottom-heavy' while shrinking on the surface. Below the surface, there were remnants of molestation, infidelity, insecurity, selfishness, greed, promiscuity, hate, jealousy...and the list

[1] National Snow and Ice Data Center, 2019

goes on. It wasn't until the Lord began warming the waters of my heart that what lied beneath melted.

The extent of what God would need to melt wasn't realized to me until an assignment in an undergraduate creative writing class. The assignment was to craft a narrative poem about an event in our lives that shaped us to be who we were at the time. My first submission was critiqued and returned with the feedback to "go deeper", as my recollection merely touched the surface. Upon deeper reflection, I uncovered the moment in my life when my trust for men diminished and my innocence was stolen, never to return.

I was six years old when a close friend of the family violated me while I attempted to show him a picture book that I would later take to school for Show and Tell. That blue picture book and "Show and Tell" began forming the iceberg that would prevent me from embracing meaningful relationships. I didn't realize how impactful this iceberg was until the Holy Spirit began to complete a work in me by revealing the manifestation of my unforgiveness as evidenced in the promiscuity that pervaded my young adult life. I sought the companionship of partners to fill an unfillable void.

I met my husband in one of the darkest moments of my life. I had multiple failed relationships; the demonic grip of promiscuity had confined me to countless soul-ties that left my esteem in the muck; and friends had recently become enemies for no obvious reason other than seasons had changed. We met on a blind date that I only accepted as a favor to a roommate, having no expectation of meeting a gentleman who was genuine in his appeal to know the 'real' me—a gift I would have been unable to give as I didn't know the 'real' me then either.

Years after meeting and marrying, we attended counseling sessions from which I realized the birth of my unforgiveness. I later wrote a letter to my violator as a means of releasing the demonic control over my life and forgive him, even though he never received the letter and never asked for forgiveness. The process of forgiving the unforgivable melted what lied dormant and activated the purging and sanctification process of the Lord.

Healing Heart:

Where does unforgiveness lie dormant in your life?

The writer of Hebrews confidently declares, "for our God is a consuming fire" (Hebrews 12:29, ESV). He responds with purging flames of fire to burn up the impurities that mar the gem He will soon display. The God we serve responds to the concerns and needs of His people by fire (1 Kings 18:24).

The prophet, Zechariah, shared the plans of the Lord to refine a remnant of His chosen people:

"And I will put this third into the fire, and refine them as one refines silver, and test them as gold is tested. They will call upon my name, and I will answer them. I will say, 'They are my people'; and they will say, 'The Lord is my God'" (Zechariah 13:9 ESV).

God responds with purging flames of fire to burn up the impurities that mar the gem He will soon display.

As the Lord transitioned His people away from idolatry and removed the stains of spiritual oppression, He enacted a purification process that would expose and remove their impurities, as well as polish their finished product. The intensity of the fire facilitates a

---

The intensity of the fire facilitates a more thorough removal of impurities ingrained in a fine stone.

---

more thorough removal of impurities ingrained in a fine stone.

Think of the Hebrew boys tossed in a furnace with a command from the king to increase the intensity of the heat because of their resiliency to stand firm on their conviction. Surely if anyone had a legitimate reason to resent and harbor unforgiveness for their oppressor, it would be these young men as they were only targeted because of their obedience to God. But in the fire was the soldering of their confidence in God's ability to deliver His people through the person of Christ as the fourth man in the fire.

The Product of 7

Among the various numerical references in the Bible, the number seven is of major importance as it represents completion and wholeness. We know that God, the Creator, completed His good work and rested on the 7th day. The prophet Elisha instructed Naaman to wash in the waters of Jordan 7 times to be healed of his affliction. Joshua led the children of Israel around Jericho 7 times on the 7th day and instructed 7 priests to blow horns as the people watched the walls that prevented their passage to come falling down before them.

The product of 7 is a whole...complete restoration and fulfillment of the promise of God. God's work in framing and filling the earth was complete in 7 days, commanding creation to be productive by being fruitful and multiplying. So, everything that would be made in the future was produced by that which He originally created. The cleansing and subsequent healing of Naaman was contingent on his obedience to the numerical instructions of the prophet, addressing the true totality of Naaman's affliction. Naaman needed to be healed of the spirit of disobedience and pride, not his obvious leprosy. Washing in the Jordan river removed the stain of pride and arrogance, and robed Naaman in humility and reverence for God—so much so that he asked for forgiveness for future moments of obedience to his master which may offend God (2 Kings 5:18). Obedience led to his acknowledgement of the frailty of man in pleasing a righteous God.

Jesus advises His disciples to, "Pay attention to yourselves! If your brother sins, rebuke him, and if he repents, forgive him, and if he sins against you seven times in the day, and turns to you seven times, saying, "I repent', you must forgive him□□□□□□□□□□□□□□" (Luke 17:3-4, ESV).

The math may appear simple, but it is difficult in application. Jesus shares that His disciples forgive a brother the seven times he sins against him and the seven times he asks for forgiveness. In another conversation with Peter, Jesus instructs his disciples to forgive seven times seven when someone offended or hurt by someone (Matthew 18:22). Simple math, right? Forgive forty-nine times and no more? Wrong. This enumeration is

---

The concept of forgiveness is rooted and grounded in God's response to His creation.

---

representative of the infinite number of times we should forgive others as we have been forgiven by the Father.

The concept of forgiveness is rooted and grounded in God's response to His creation. The Apostle Paul reminds us that our gracious God displayed His infinite love and forgiveness for us that while we were sinners He devised a plan for our redemption and restoration (Romans 5:8). So even when we were unrepentant, unworthy, and unrighteous, God forgave us and sought to rebuild a relationship with us.

The extent to which God forgave us was so extreme He commissioned His servant, Hosea, to become a living example. The Lord instructed Hosea, "Go, take to yourself a wife of whoredom and have children of whoredom, for the land commits great whoredom by forsaking the Lord" (Hosea 1:2 ESV). Hosea obliged and witnessed the infidelity of his beloved wife, just as God sits high and watches the countless times we fail on our promise to faithfully love and serve Him. But beyond unfaithfulness stood love. God instructs Hosea to embrace his wife and love her once again, despite her indiscretions.

How do we justify our refusal to forgive others when God never hesitates to forgive us? We rationalize our refusal with the fact that we are not God and highlight our many imperfections as a crutch to strengthen our argument. But this fact is the perfect counterargument to why our righteous and holy God should not forgive us. It all comes down to love: His love for us, despite our disregard for Him. The Bible reassures us that this love is so strong and permanent that nothing can separate us from it (Romans 8:38-39).

It all comes down to love: God's love for us, despite our disregard for Him.

I didn't fully understand this concept until the Lord transformed me into a wife for my husband...years after being married. Throughout our early years of marriage, I prided myself on being the spouse who knew the recipe for creating the perfect marriage because I watched my parents do it for 30 years. I constantly held my husband to an unfair standard set by who I thought my father was as a husband to my mother—never realizing I only knew and saw the picture they drew for me, their baby girl, not the complexities that come with loving someone through the most unlovable circumstances.

I was soon faced with situations that would test the love I professed and require my husband and I to jointly draw the image of a marriage unique to our own canvas. Instead of me asking God to change my husband, I asked the Lord to change me...and make me the wife he needed. Unbeknownst to me, he was praying the same prayer for himself.

I saw forgiveness as a gift of grace I generously gave as a token of my love, just as God did for me. Some may wonder, "well if I keep forgiving certain indiscretions, won't my spouse continue engaging in this behavior?" The answer to this question is in your response to another question, "Do you trust God with your heart?". If you trust God with your heart, then you know that He would not allow the enemy to get the victory from your obedience and humility. God won't make a fool out of you...and you've got to believe that! Allow yourself to become vulnerable.

Healing Heart:

Do you trust God with your heart? How do you demonstrate that trust?

Me Too

Not only is forgiving others a requirement but forgiving yourself is essential too.

The Apostle Paul reminds us that all of us have sinned and fallen short of God's expectations, that none of us is righteous apart from the work of the Holy Spirit within us (Romans 3:23). The astonishing news flash is that we are not perfect beings. Imagine that, we are made in the image of God but lack perfection. If we were perfect, we would have no need for God's intervention.

The beauty of embracing our imperfections is the acknowledgement of God's grace to love and forgive us beyond our humanity. As humans we will misstep and commit unintentional offenses--it's in our nature, as descendants of the first Adam (1 Corinthians 15:25). But after receiving God's Spirit through our acceptance of Jesus Christ, we are transformed into spiritual beings no longer slaves to our human nature. We are no longer enjoined to the mistakes of our past and we are free to forgive ourselves for succumbing to the demands of our human nature.

The Word of God affirms, "For as high as the heavens are above the earth, so great is his steadfast love toward those who fear him; as far as the east is from the west, so far does he remove our transgressions from us" (Psalms 103:11-12, ESV). If God separated us from the sin that would forever separate us from Him, why do we feel the need to reconnect to that sin and continue with the old identity and pattern of behaviors that enslaved us? We are free, and whom the Son has declared to be free is indeed free (John 8:38).

There are times, however, when we are unaware of the patterns of behavior that orchestrate our desire to fixate on the mistakes of our past. I didn't realize the extent to which I had not forgiven myself from the years of reckless behavior brought on by my failure to unearth the roots of childhood molestation. I was a married woman and mother of small children before the Lord exposed the patterns of behavior that prevented me from not only seeing myself as God saw me, but through the eyes of my husband. It was difficult for me to accept his compliments and gestures of affection because I viewed them as precursors for salacious debt repayments. I would automatically subconsciously think, "*Surely, he is only complimenting me because he wants intimacy from me*". Not only was this grossly inaccurate, it was an unfair assessment of the man that vowed to love and honor me as Christ loved and honored His bride, the church. I needed complete detachment from the transgressions that labeled me "loose", "promiscuous", and "unworthy", and I needed to connect with God's words that renamed me, "virtuous", "righteous", and "loved".

Once the root of my behavior was revealed, I had the power to stop the pattern and break the cycle so not only could I heal, but my marriage could heal too. I was able to finally receive my husband's sincere expression of love in its purest form and slowly work towards reciprocating this affection.

Are you ready to stop the negative pattern of behavior that controls your self- perception, self-esteem and your interactions with others? Start by forgiving yourself. Ask God to expose the areas of your life that harbor pain, shame, and resentment. Ask for His forgiveness...and then forgive yourself. Accept your human imperfections yet recognize God's purpose in the painful and disgraceful moments of our lives—juxtaposing grace and mercy against judgement and condemnation. As new creations in Christ, the old ways and indiscretions of our past have passed away because everything has become new: new outlook, new image, new roadmap...a new you!

Finally, reject thoughts that oppose God's view of you. Set your mind and pattern your new behavior after that which is, "... is true, whatever is honorable, whatever is just, whatever is pure, whatever is lovely, whatever is commendable" (Philippians 4:8, ESV). Let these things lay the foundation for your self-love and healing.

Healing Heart:

What is true, honorable, just, pure, lovely and commendable in your life that deserves your attention?

Cementing the Cracks

Take a step towards being healed from UNFORGIVENESS by engaging in the reflection activity below.

Read: Colossians 3:13, Matthew 6:14-15, Ephesians 4:31-32, 1 John 1:9, Acts 3:19, and Micah 7:18-19

Respond: Who or what do you need to forgive to move forward in your life? How will you begin that process?

Release: Write action steps that will help you develop a new pattern of behavior to control your self- perception, self-esteem and your interactions with others.

Prayer:

Heavenly Father heal me from the yoke of unforgiveness. Untie me from the strings of my past that have strangled my relationships, self-esteem and perception of Your love for me. Help me to release the moments in my life when others have done wrong to me and I have done wrong to others, including myself. Change the way I view situations so I can always see Your hand working on my behalf and for my good. Lastly, teach me how to love You, others and myself without conditions and false expectations, but true sincerity of the heart.

Final Thoughts

Many readers stepped into the pages of this book desiring to uncover the secrets to healing obvious afflictions that challenge our physical and emotional health. But what you hopefully received were scripturally backed insights into our responses to the moments or events in our lives that change us.

Prior to the release of this book, the Lord saw fit to place my family and I in one of the most challenging seasons of our lives. My father was diagnosed with Prostate Cancer and my aunt diagnosed with Pancreatic Cancer within months of each other, both of whom were being cared for by my mother. To watch your loved ones physically fight to live and kill that which secretly attempts to kill them, opened my spiritual eyes to the foundational element of healing: our response to trials and afflictions.

As beings formed from the clay of the ground, we are subject to the physical consequences of sin. The book of Romans 8 records that even creation awaits the day of Christ's return so it can be healed and redeemed of the consequences of sin. So, we also wait: wait when we are diagnosed with cancer, wait when our bank accounts are empty, wait when our hearts are broken and wait when it seems like chaos has its free reign.

"For the creation was subjected to futility, not willingly, but because of him who subjected it, in hope that the creation itself will be set free from its bondage to corruption and obtain the freedom of the glory of the children of God" (Romans 8:20-21, ESV).

To get caught up in the physical manifestation of that which afflicts us only touches the surface. To receive true healing, we must address the inner spiritual conflicts that control our response to the inevitable physical afflictions that attack us. Sure, my family will continue to pray for the cancer that has attacked our loved one's bodies to be eradicated and for their bodies to fully recover, but we are realizing that our prayers and focus must go beyond the obvious physical need and address the spiritual.

"And do not fear those who kill the body but cannot kill the soul. Rather fear him who can destroy both soul and body in hell" (Matthew 10:28, ESV).

Are you whole and well, spiritually (even if your physical body is afflicted)? What are the spiritual areas of your life that need healing? Addressing these questions empowers you to handle the many adversities tied to the consequences of sin. Throughout this season, I watched my mom become a caregiver to two people she adored stricken with cancer. There were days of multiple trips to doctors' offices at hospitals on the opposite sides of town, days of which the physical pain incited verbal assaults, days of frustration in dealing with medical billing and prescription pricing, and many days of sleeplessness. But, in those days I saw an unimaginable outpouring of patience and love, which led me to wonder, "how on earth is my elderly mom handling all of this all at once and at her age?". It was because God was performing a work in her that would heal her spirit and soul, empowering her to approach each day with a God-inspired outlook on the opportunities that awaited them all. That's right, the day's afflictions were no longer challenges but opportunities for God's glory to reign. So, a cancer diagnosis was an opportunity for God through his servants (doctors, pastors, etc.) to demonstrate His ability to physically and spiritually heal us in our most vulnerable state.

Psalm 34: 19 reminds us that, "Many are the afflictions of the righteous, but the Lord delivers him out of them all" (ESV).

In closing, let us be encouraged by the concluding words of the Apostle Paul in 2 Corinthians 4:7-18:

"But we have this treasure in jars of clay, to show that the surpassing power belongs to God and not to us. We are afflicted in every way, but not crushed; perplexed, but not driven to despair; persecuted, but not forsaken; struck down, but not destroyed; always carrying in the body the death of Jesus, so that the life of Jesus may also be manifested in our bodies. For we who live are always being given over to death for Jesus' sake, so that the life of Jesus also may be manifested in our mortal flesh. So, death is at work in us, but life in you. Since we have the same spirit of faith according to what has been written, "I believed, and so I spoke," we also believe, and so we also speak, knowing that he who raised the Lord Jesus will raise us also with Jesus and bring us with you into his presence. For it is all for your sake, so that as grace extends to more and more people it may increase thanksgiving, to the glory of God. So, we do not lose heart. Though our outer self is wasting away, our inner self is being renewed day by day. For this light momentary affliction is preparing for us an eternal weight of glory beyond all comparison, as we look not to the things that are seen but to the things that are unseen. For the things that are seen are transient, but the things that are unseen are eternal."

ABOUT THE AUTHOR

Pastor Youmone Berrien is a passionate millennial leader and the co-founder of Commissioned By Christ Outreach Church. She is a veteran professional educator, wife and mother of four boys. She is the co-author of *Grace In One*, a 2018 book released to share the journey of her family's testimony of God's grace during the birth and death of her daughter.

CPSIA information can be obtained
at www.ICGtesting.com
Printed in the USA
BVHW040918230121
598560BV00017B/608

9 781090 706508